Survival:
Trees, Tides, Song

poems by

Marjorie Moorhead

Finishing Line Press
Georgetown, Kentucky

Survival:
Trees, Tides, Song

Copyright © 2019 by Marjorie Moorhead
ISBN 978-1-63534-923-8 First Edition
All rights reserved under International and Pan-American Copyright Conventions. No part of this book may be reproduced in any manner whatsoever without written permission from the publisher, except in the case of brief quotations embodied in critical articles and reviews.

Publisher: Leah Maines

Editor: Christen Kincaid

Cover Art: Marjorie Moorhead

Author Photo: Marjorie Moorhead

Cover Design: Leah Huete

Printed in the USA on acid-free paper.
Order online: www.finishinglinepress.com
          also available on amazon.com

Author inquiries and mail orders:
Finishing Line Press
P. O. Box 1626
Georgetown, Kentucky 40324
U. S. A.

Table of Contents

Choir 1
Starlight in My Pocket 2
Join Me 3
East Thetford, VT 4
The Wisdom of Geese 5
Thank You Mary Oliver 6
Us 7
All of a Sudden, Just Like That 8
Turtle Island Microfiber 9
Because an Invitation… 10
Borders 11
Rat-a-Tat-Rain 12
Marcescence 13
Surviving 14
Wandering the Anthropocene 15
Tides 16
Walking, Wondering, Telling a Tale 17
(Villanelle) For My Planet 18
Tragedy Triolet where were you when the bombs dropped? 19
Things I've Seen in the Anthropocene (Make Me
    Wanna Holler) 20
Swallows at Canaan St. Lake 22
Hearing the Song 23

*This collection of poems is dedicated to
my family,
my teachers/friends,
and the memory of
Jorge Soto, Scott Eddins, Deneal Amos.*

the Welsh phrase "dod ynôl at fy nghoed"—meaning "to return to a balanced state of mind"— translates literally as "to return to my trees"
Robert Macfarlane

Choir

I sing in a Forrest Choir.
It's me and the trees. Tall slim trunks standing in line.
Soprano, Alto, Tenor, Bass. Birch, Maple, Apple, Pine.
With wind as our Leader; harmonies soar.

When I was young, I knew the trees as friends.
My gaze through green boughs to blue sky brought knowledge of certain connection.
Nature and I were one and the same, and that same was Perfection.
But, leaving childhood brings doubts and clouds. Certainty ends.

Happy with outsiders, I was drawn to a gifted, afflicted artist who,
in the language of trees, was first "marcescent" (withering, yet holding on), then
"deciduous" (shedding all). Witnessing this unravel seemed when
life was hardest. Finding the way of my own survival, new challenges grew.

Now, wind is Choir Leader; clouds, audience. In concert, harmonies soar.
Tall trunks, textured with bark; vertical, gate-like, bridge to the sky.
Tonal humming. Vibration. A song key tunes our hearts. Time to fly!
Now, I sing in a Forrest Choir.

Starlight in My Pocket

A song I'm learning says, "Catch a falling star;"
it says, "put in your pocket." A clue:
keep it there for when needed; when things look blue.

Keep it, for when troubles start growing,
creating a fright.
The song says, "and they just might."

Troubles are easy to forget without trying,
the lyrics say; all that's needed: "a pocketful of starlight."
Who's got starlight?! Will it help when I'm crying?

I keep a rock from the beach in my pocket.
Smooth, to rub. Silky soft surface.
Dissipates worry. Works; don't knock it.

Smoothed by the sea, not a scratch or scar.
Is it my "starlight?" Gives comfort;
like music, while driving the car.

Trees whizz by. I sing out, at the top of my lungs
releasing anxiety; things that have stung.
Not kept in reserve "for a rainy day,"

this orb, too, in my pocket, helps worries fall away.
An everyday tool. With me while I cruise,
in car, or on foot, singing the Blues.

Join Me

Joinery. Mending, melding, welding
back together.

Seems the only thing saving me
these days is trees.

The fact of trees. How they are;
their particular presence.

Saves me from separating into parts.
Bits that could float apart or

burst outward at some seam.
Bolting off in opposite directions

away from center;
from core.

Trees stand tall;
stand through it all

quietly, majestically, offering
their essence.

Strong trunks; textured bark;
leaves either there, or not there on lace-intricate branches.

Join me.
Let's stand with trees

to gather;
collect.

East Thetford, VT

Walking saved me years ago
Walking the same route every day
Day after day season after season.

Early morning; mid-day; dusk

It was only a mile or so
down to the farm and back
a flat road off the main road; probably once a train-rail.

Grasses; corn; clouds

Backdrop-sky for stone house, wood barn
tall stalks, big trees, lilacs.
At sunset simple silhouettes framing pink and orange-purple swaths.

Smells; wind; birds

My steps, my thoughts;
the rhythm of stride, breath.
Watching and noting details. What changes; what stays constant.

Dirt; puddles; tracks

Relationship with land can be just a road
claimed with each footstep.
You know it, because you walk it.

Repetition; observation; devotion

The Wisdom of Geese

Do they know, before they go?
That they'll stick together;
watching out for one another?
A feathered band of brothers-and-others.

Are they willing to circle the wagon
if one becomes a drag on
group flight?
Such a beautiful sight,

the shaped formation.
Flying in unison to shared destination.
Soaring as one to reach far-away shelter;
fleeing not "shelter in place" and "active shooter;"

they're seeking climate that can sustain their group.
Cooperation, camaraderie's the coup.
Do they know, before they go
away from ice, sleet, snow, what it takes to let peace grow?

Thank You Mary Oliver

You say them so well; so clearly;
Simple and holy things

Weighted with beauty yet light in simplicity, impermanence
Amazing in their eternal return

Steadfast, brief; cherished gifts in your arms
Rose petals, falling snow, a shimmering moth

Held to our view, praises sung, and lovingly set free
You place us in the line-up as partners

Precious, and leaving
We celebrate togetherness

Us

Clutterer, stutterer,
flutter flutter; o.c.d.
you and me.

Birds of a feather;
do we fit together?

I help you find a way;
you help me;
we play.

Years pass;
wrinkled, bent,
bald, spent.

Won't relent; right to the end
I will depend on us.

All of a Sudden; Just Like That...

Just like that, leaves are red in swaths
tinted by a perennial brush.
Autumn hues orange, gold, yellowed.
All of a sudden, it's cold in morning's hush
and dark. Fog hangs in valleys until the chill has mellowed.

Just like that, sun seems precious.
A limited commodity to be hoarded.
An aid in the battle against scarcity.
All of a sudden, geese fly overhead, squadron sorted,
sailing the clouds toward warmth, squawking commands with levity.

Just like that, I tug for my share of sheet
in morning's chill, instead of pushing it off
to avoid the humid sweat of August.
All of a sudden, t-shirts aren't enough;
long pants are pulled from drawers; thick sweaters become a must.

Just like that my little blond-haired boys look like men.
At the table, my husband and I shadowed with long silence.
Parents seem brittle like branches; dry, and primed to snap.
All of a sudden, life's like a movie; scenes gone by in sequence.
Family pets grown old. I rock them, our small moments and big events
piled in my lap.

Turtle Island Microfiber

The radio tells me this morning,
in voices kind and concerned,

there are particles of plastic in Lake Champlain
so small, they can't be filtered by treatment plants.

"Micro plastic trash" they called it.
("Punk Rock band" my ears amuse).

This plastic from fleece-wear
"will merge with our food chain", is announced.

We will eat plasticated fish
from laundering our fine-threaded plastic shirts.

My son, visiting home from college, has my head spinning
trying to keep up with all his words for environmental and social tragedy.

Apparently, we are trying to repossess
ourselves of our humanity

away from psycho technology
in the Anthropocene.

I am glad his generation is trying
to figure it out because

I want my children, and theirs,
to know sparkling water that hosts creatures who

co-habit with us and provide sustenance
that is clean and pure.

Water they can dip their toes into and want to plunge further.
Nutritious air that lungs can consume with passion.

Will that story be a memory told,
of an ancient dream, of an island called "Turtle?"

Because an Invitation...

Because I'm up before the dawn,
I see rosy clouds appear as sun breaks.
Because it is late November,

all is couched in a hazy cold moisture cluster;
festering, gathering, waiting for weight
to bring it down as snow.

Few leaves hanging on.
Most have hit the earth,
skittered and clattered dryly away.

Now tree skeletons stand tall and proud,
showing beautiful silhouettes
on a cold air screen.

Will they get a blanket?
How thick will it be?
A many snowflake'd quilt, joined in unique pattern.

Because I worry about such things,
I think about the shoveling out,
and the shuttering in.

Because it seems like old school survival;
boots pulled over wool,
ear flaps, gloves, scarves,
tissues and hot soup at hand.

Will the frail and infirm survive?
To be warmed by Spring,
and hear it's song?
Because an invitation is on its way
for the hardy.

Borders

For the second time in a short while
I find myself sitting under rain drops.
The sound sweeps in and away as a hard pattering
like hooves of battalion horses moving through. A windblown storm cloud.

Previously: a steady pounding coupled with thunder and lightning.
I did not feel threatened then; though later came reports hail had fallen!
There was a terror attack in London. My sister and brother-in-law are there.
I find myself thinking it's for the best my son is moving from Manhattan
to Queens.

We could be under rain drops anywhere. Tragedy visits anywhere.
Where do we find ourselves? Borders in our minds.
What we could fathom and what we could not.
Rising sea levels. Depleting ice caps. Dividing lines.

Rat-a-Tat Rain

Sitting in a room where raindrops reverb.
Pinging hard, like machine gun fire today.
Disturb pitter-patter rapid-fire style.
Bump stock speed: no delay.

Picking off leaves one by one.
Red, golden, orange, brown.
Torn from branch and stem; each bullet drop
tears one down.

Shapes gather to form a blanket, wet.
Lay atop Autumn grass and let
death's gleam shimmer and wink.

The joke: Winter must come. Don't think
it won't. All will slow and fester;
in small places sequester.

Huddle for warmth and shelter!
The Ice Queen cometh; we've all felt her.
"Shelter in Place!" "Rat-a-tat" there it is again!

In meditation; legs crossed, spine straight
that's when I hear it: harsh rain.
Usually too busy to let it into my brain,

in silence and full presence
I hear the drops above.
An introduction to this Season's essence:

Light to dark,
fluid to frozen, active to hibernating,
abundant to empty; stark.

Marcescence

Not unlike marcescent leaves;
huddled snow-covered stones of a wall;

dry hydrangea balls, old as withering fists;
crumpled, as paper, blown loose from stem,
rolling with the wind like tumbleweed.

Not unlike sidewalk puddles, coming from frozen ice and snow,
maybe salted by sidewalk plow-sweeps of early morning commute,
reflecting up the sky.

The single fencepost-glove; stiff finger pointing
skyward, impaled, waiting for ownership.
Dropped by a pram-pushing mother, or a legging-clad runner,
momentarily warmed by the sun; by activity,
hanging on to hope of reunification.

Not unlike these late winter things,
I wait, yearning for Spring.

Surviving

There's a fog outside.
Thickness in the air.
It's three in the afternoon. Not yet dark
but you feel dusk is near.

What's left of the snow is heavy.
Almost water, but not. White; still holding form,
it slides from roofs in slabs; edge-curling sheaths.
Drips from edges into gutters onto valleys where roofs meet.

Beneath the weighty evaporating blanket of white:
mud. Brown grasses. Old leaves.
Waiting to be washed away by Spring rains—
still a few months off—that will beckon

the green we all await. Winter was hard.
Cold hearts;
blind eyes;
wrong directions;

erosion of foundations. We all need to rebuild;
restructure. Mend and improve.
The process must be inclusive; respectful; dedicated.
Our garden must be planted with

seeds of strength and beauty
the likes of which have not yet shown their face
to the sky. It is our job to nurture this. To
guide, protect, cajole it forth.

Our garden.
Our future.
Our legacy.
Survival.

Wandering the Anthropocene

LED lights flickering
Microwaves emitting

Surveilling satellites vie for air ways
With cell phone frequencies

Rubble and soot-filled air
Like the 9/11 toxins everywhere

Devastated environments
Endless wars; careless industries

Once thriving communities dying
Bleached coral; flattened Mosul

Plastics and nuclear isotopes
Failed reactors; failed states

Failure to thrive
Shrinking ice; drought; floodwater coursing

Created scarcity
Our byproduct of greed

Seeds genetically modified
Mismanaged soil toxically fertilized

Humans displaced
Species disappeared

Searching for authenticity
With freedom from techno-tyranny

Striving for existence reclaimed
Community found in terms un-dictated

Kickstart organic motivation
Individuals must make the proclamation
to flourish

Tides

Are we tied to a tide's ebb and flow?
Is there Balance; Justice in our universe?
In a life-time, do you reap what you sow?
Does the debris from our living recede as time's tides reverse?
Each wave brings in a crop of sand.
For inspection: bits of shell, glass, wood, shimmering scales;
remnants of a below-the-surface sea-ruled world at hand.
Are there clues to point us toward Justice on our above-ground trails?

Are there clues to point us toward Justice on earth-bound trails?
Remnants of a below-the-surface sea-ruled world are at hand
for our inspection. Bits of shell, glass, wood, shimmering scales
delivered in each wave's crop of sand.
Does the debris of our living recede as Time's tide reverses?
In a life-time, do we reap what we've sown?
If there is balance, justice in our universes.
Are we tied to the ebb and flow we've known?

Walking, Wondering, Telling a Tale

Spiky pods hang from Pine branches in a line dance,
like decoration for their holiday;
or lights, strung around edges of a cafe.

No need for scientific nomenclature;
in my mind, simply "pods" is sufficient .
Except, really it isn't.

Doesn't tell you specific nature:
light brown colored bumpy covers, mace-like on an oval shaped body;
dangling orbs hanging in rows along a vine, hugging it's host-tree.

Names have this reason. When I say "Pine" (from "Pinaceae": of the conifers' family tree)
you know of green needles, in each season covering branches in bristles;
you can smell a scent; see clustered cones shaped like missiles.

A Poets' world mixes words with notions.
Questions that surface are pondered and turned;
churned into phrases using appellations we've learned.

If I wonder at beauty, clarity, majesty, rarity;
if I see leaf, tree, shoreline, shell, mountain-shapes, moon-glimmer,
I will ask, in verse rhyming or not, what is it I may tell, poignantly, that can't be forgot?

Mythical, prophetic, perhaps cautionary, I might tell a tale of ice.
Weave twinkling words into a story; use the words "shuckle," "shimmer" or grimmer: "melting sheets, going once, twice, thrice…"

(Villanelle) For My Planet

Treat your home with love; it will sustain you.
Unattended, webbing can tear.
A net's weave is strong when its connections are true.

Our actions have changed things more than we knew.
We haven't treated our surroundings with care.
Treat your home with love; it will sustain you.

Stories are told using many a hue;
facts about deeds not always laid bare.
A net's weave is strong only when its connections are true.

The lies we were told by greedy oligarchs grew.
Their practice of depletion and pillage for profit, not fair.
Treat our home with love; it will sustain you.

Let us rip open the veil and see through.
We need all be invested in our habitat's fare.
A net's weave is strong when its connections are true.

Time has come for action that's new.
Create stewardship in which we all have a share.
Treat Home with love; it will sustain you.
A net's weave's as strong as its connections are true.

Tragedy Triolet
where were you when the bombs dropped?

I was watching PBS, when the bombs were dropped.
A show about music, which spoke to my heart.
Little did I know, much-pried Pandora's Box-lid had popped.
I was watching a tv show when the bombs were dropped.
Pillowed surroundings quiet, normal; nothing routine had stopped.
On the show, poet-singer protest-warriors strumming their art.
I danced; snapped fingers at my screen, not yet knowing bombs were dropped.
Marvin Gaye, Dylan, Garcia's music spoke to my heart.

Things I've Seen in the Anthropocene (Make Me Wanna Holler)

Makes me want to scream. Makes me want to holler.
Like the Marvin Gaye song.*
Feeling sad, and mean, in the anthropocene.

Witness to bird remains; their shapes filled-in
with plastic trash consumed.
Pecked from once pristine sands.

Now, our oceans wash ashore
plastic waste galore.
Excrement of our life style;

our love relation with plastic straws,
plastic cups. Styrofoam take-fast-
food-out mentality has made

a wasteland our reality.
We're strip mined, clear-cut, fracked and drilled.
Big Oil, Big Pharma, Big Agra thrilled.

We've spread pesticides; isotopes.
Bleached our coral; poisoned our bees.
Backed into a corner;

no hopes; on our knees.
But, there are those on the outskirts
thinking outside a box or screen,

who know re-focus is in order.
New paradigm required.
In their hands is held my hopes

for change; for salvation.
They—the unfettered ones—have the motivation
to flourish in community;

to reclaim with impunity the
reins that have steered so far askew.
Pull us back into focus on what is good, and true.

Make me want to scream. Please.
Make me want to holler—
for joy.

* Inner City Blues (Make Me Wanna Holler). Marvin Gaye, What's Going On, 1971

Swallows at Canaan St. Lake

A clear sharp sky.
Clouds in isolated attendance.
Stand-alone puffs fully formed and weighted.

One choreographed moment, each fluff lined up;
a staircase of stepping stones,
one to another, and beyond.

In a patch of sky, free of cloud;
the Swallows.
Meeting on high, soaring together.

Each white belly catching the sun's light,
reflecting so brightly, as a twinkle on the string
of bulbs dressing park trees and cafe walls.

A sparkling flash, bright for a nano-second
as the Swallow's body turns
in the wind of its flight.

Like little Penguins in extreme-bonsai miniature,
their black-winged white bodies play in the air
as if on ice, or in the sea.

Glinting, glinting,
with each turn toward the sun.
Every wink of white exposure a belly dance.

Blinking neon light-like reminder:
we play on this earth;
our flight-dance made together.

Hearing the Song

Deep red Cardinal in a tree,
like a sailor in ship's crow's nest.
Piercing notes from open throated song
float to changing winds at his chest.

Red Cardinal—do you know White Rhino is gone?
"Sudan;" last male of his breed.
Will you sing him a monody;
mark his passing in your prosody; the sounded urgency we need?

*

Painted Sea Anemones, floating in currents
off British Columbia. Like blossoms below the surface,
on display.
Forcefully fed nutrients in Ocean's swells; multi-colored;
they resemble a flower-shop's vibrant bouquet.

Great Pacific Garbage Patch (GPGP);
a trash vortex, between Cali. and Hawaii.
Riding a gyre, bright colored plastic shards
and fishing nets form this multi-pieced barge,
looming as an island of debris.
If, like surface-coating oil, dark and slick,
it shadowed the bouquet anemones,
who'd sing their elegy; lament their getting sick?

*

An Elephant gives birth surrounded by others circling in,
to protect the calf. A fortress of swinging trunks,
wide flat hooves, flapping grey ears, wrinkled skin.
Do they sense extinction lurking? Like White Rhino Sudan,
will they vanish too, in coming years?

New England has lost Eastern Cougar. Vanished; gone; "Ghost Cat."
Our "Catamount/Puma/Mountain Lion" will never again be seen.
Species' extinction is rampant. Imagine that.
An escalating crisis of the Anthropocene.

*

High atop tree boughs, red Cardinal trilling, claiming his spot,
joins a wild chorus, singing Earth's praises.
Red-brown mother, in carefully crafted cup-nest,
joins, with her own lyric phrases.

We should listen to Cardinals' song. Elephant's ways.
Anemones being nourished in Ocean's currents.
Pray over vanished Rhino's bone.
Remember the roars of Big Cats who perish.
We cannot exist on this planet alone.
We should listen. We should cherish.

ACKNOWLEDGMENTS

Grateful acknowledgement is made to the anthologies and journals where some of these poems appeared previously, possibly with a different title, or in different form. These include:

Indolent Books' *Countdown to World AIDS Day 2017**

Birchsong: Poetry Centered in VT, Vol.II (4/2018, edited by Alice Wolf Gilborn, et al., The Blueline Press)

Indolent Books' *What Rough Beast**

Rising Phoenix Review

A Change of Climate (12/2017, edited by Sam Illingworth and Dan Simpson, benefitting The Environmental Justice Foundation)

*Special thanks to Michael Broder

Thank you to Catherine O'Brian, for early encouragement.
Thank you to Joni Cole for writing inspiration.
Thank you to Leah Maines for selecting this collection of work for publication.

Always a quiet observer; a native New Englander, **Marjorie Moorhead** moved, after college, to live and work in the art world of NYC in the early 1980's, where she met the artist Jorge Soto Sanchez. Eventually, they lived together in VT, until his untimely death from AIDS. From there, Marjorie was set on a journey of discovery, connecting her with many teachers, and eventually emboldening her to become a Poet. Mountains, rivers, woods, ocean, the Northern New England change of season, are all present in her writing. Marjorie turns the critical, yet all-embracing eye of a survivor on all she filters into her poetry. She hopes to continue sharing her work, bearing witness, in the company of brave and creative people, who strive for openness, truth, and beauty.

Marjorie feels fortunate to be included in many anthologies. In particular, one of climate change poems, benefiting the Environmental Justice Foundation. Also, a collection from poets in and near to VT. She has had many poems online, and is happy that the sites who published her work value commentary from a variety of voices on our current state of affairs as a nation and society. Marjorie is proud to have performed her poem, *What If...*, at an event raising awareness of domestic and sexual violence. She meets regularly with her group, 4th Friday Poets.

Everything meaningful in her life is supported by the love Marjorie gets and has for her husband, sons, sisters, and parents.

www.ingramcontent.com/pod-product-compliance
Lightning Source LLC
LaVergne TN
LVHW041513070426
835507LV00012B/1543